How to Make Money at Craft Shows

Art Market and Craft Fair Tips & Tricks

Mallory Whitfield

ISBN: 1535086610

ISBN-13: 978-1535086615

Have you ever wanted to sell your handmade crafts or artwork at local craft fairs, but have no idea where to start? Or maybe you've taken the first step and have tried selling your art at a craft show or two, but now you're looking for ideas on how to sell more, how to make your booth more appealing to customers, and where to find more venues to sell your handmade goods?

You've come to the right place! I've been selling my own handmade creations, as well as the work of other artists, at a variety of craft shows and other events around New Orleans and beyond since 2004. I've learned a lot of lessons the hard way, and now I'm sharing them here with you so that you can learn from my experiences!

In this book, I'll cover the basics of getting started selling at craft fairs, as well as how to design a great looking booth, how to give outstanding customer service and sell more, and even how to find and create additional events at which to sell your work.

Let's get started!

Mallory Whitfield

www.MissMalaprop.com

CONTENTS

1 DEFINING YOUR TARGET MARKET.

First things first, in order to find the best craft shows for you, you'll need to define your target market. Knowing this will help you focus on the shows that will be most profitable for you.

Depending on where you live, the types of shows and how to find them may vary. I always get a little jealous of folks who live in places where there are bigger alternative craft shows geared towards the types of crafts I'm into. Being from the South, where there are a variety of church craft fairs and more traditional "country" craft shows, I've learned the hard way that my quirky style doesn't really fit with that type of show. Finding the shows that are right for you requires a lot of trial and error. But if you can focus on who your ideal customer is (and chances are they're a lot like you), you can begin to focus on the types of shows that will be most profitable for you and your art.

Start thinking about what type of art you make. What kind of person would it appeal to? Think about the person that you envision buying your art. What does he or she look like? What do they do for living? What is their lifestyle? This task of defining your target market is so important on so many levels of your business. It will help you figure out what shows will be profitable for you, and it will help you determine how to effectively market your business.

What is a target market?

Your target market is your core group of customers. Even if you sell to all different types of people, you probably make most of your money off of one demographic. For me, that is women between the ages of 25-34 with a college education who have a disposable income and prefer smaller boutiques and independent brands over shopping malls and big chain stores. (See how specific I was? Get as specific as possible about who your target market is!)

Why should I care?

If you not only know exactly who your target market is, but also where they hang out (online and in real life), and how many of them there are, you can make more accurate financial projections for your business. You can save money on marketing and avoid wasted booth fees by focusing on the shows that are most likely to attract your target customer, instead of wasting time and money on shows that attract the wrong type of crowd for your product.

How do I know who my target market is?

If you've already been selling your work for a while, whether online or at craft shows, you can figure this out by looking back at your past sales. Are your customers mostly men or women? Where do they live? Have they dropped any hints about their lifestyles via customer comments? Sometimes even email addresses can tell a story about your customers' likes or dislikes.

Surveys are another great way to find out who the majority of your customers are. Encourage survey participation by offering up a prize or special discount to your customers. Survey Monkey (*www.surveymonkey.com*) offers both free and paid tools for surveying your customers.

If you're just starting out, you'll have to do a little more guessing. But in most cases, your target market ends up being a whole lot like you. Sometimes it can be helpful to create a character, an actual imaginary person, who is the epitome of your target market. Having this person in your mind when you're booking your next show or creating a new product will help you to focus on what's profitable.

How can I use this info to make me more money?

Once you know exactly who your ideal customer is, you can stop wasting money on shows that aren't right for you. Request information from craft show organizers about the crowd they usually attract. If they can't provide demographics, try to find out the information from fellow artists who have done the show in the past. If those demographics don't fall in line with your key market, move on.

You can also analyze census data (find United States census data at www.census.gov) to figure out exactly how many people are in your target market. You can even get an idea of how many potential customers you have in your own zip code, or in the zip code of a new craft show you'd like to try out, via the website *www.City-Data.com*.

Defining your target market is a really important part of your business. Knowing who your primary customer is will inform almost all of your business decisions. If you don't have this figured out yet, now is the time to get started!

Let's define your target market.

DO THIS NOW!

- ➢ What does your ideal customer look like?
- ➢ Are they primarily male or female?
- ➢ What is their age range?
- ➢ What is the highest level of education they've completed?
- ➢ How much money do they make a year?
- ➢ Do they have children?
- ➢ What types of websites and magazines do they read?
- ➢ Where do they like to shop?
- ➢ What stores and brands do they like?
- ➢ How do they spend their weekends?
- ➢ What types of events and activities do they attend?

2 WHERE TO FIND GOOD SHOWS.

An absolutely invaluable resource in terms of finding good shows is your fellow crafter.

I will often ask fellow crafter friends their opinions on shows that they've done in the past, and I am always willing to share my own opinions when they ask me. Other artists may not always be willing to share the details of their very best shows, but I've found that artists are generally more than willing to talk shop and love to share details about which shows they like, or don't like, and why.

How do I find fellow artists if I'm just starting out?

Try searching Facebook for local artists and craft groups to connect with. Etsy Teams (*www.etsy.com/teams*) are another great place to connect with local crafters.

Once you start doing craft shows, be sure to talk to the artists in the booths near you. Crafters often enjoy swapping info about past and upcoming shows during their current events. While you're setting up or breaking down your display during your next show, try chatting up your neighbors about their opinions on different local events and see if they have recommendations.

Many crafters also list their upcoming, and sometimes past, events on their websites or in their Etsy profiles. You can use this as a tool in your search as well. Sometimes I browse the events pages of other artists' websites, and if I see an upcoming event that they are participating in that I'm curious about, I will email them to see if they are willing to share details on it, and how I might register for it.

Online resources to find craft shows.

Craftlister, Unanimous Craft, FestivalNet and ZAPPlication are all great places to start your search:

> Craftlister (*www.craftlister.com*) features a variety of events, big and small, and many long-running events include reviews written by previous vendors. Some listings are more complete than others, as some are pulled from various online sources such as newspapers and other event listing sites, and some events are user-submitted. A free account on Craftlister lets you see only a certain amount of upcoming listings, but you can donate money to receive a full membership, or you can also add your own reviews and event listings to get a temporary membership upgrade, which will allow you to see everything.

> Unanimous Craft (*www.unanimouscraft.com*) is an all-around great resource for any craft artist, but they offer a calendar section in their members-only area which lists craft-related events of all varieties from around the world.

> FestivalNet (*festivalnet.com*) has been around since 1996 and features an extensive listing of music festivals, craft shows, art festivals and fairs in the U.S. and Canada.

> ZAPP (*www.zapplication.org*) is "a one-stop universal online application system that allows

artists to submit and manage applications for participating art shows, festivals and fairs." From what I've found, ZAPP seems to be for bigger, more established shows, often the kind with more expensive booth and application fees. These types of shows are typically juried, which means that a panel of judges will view all of the applications they receive and vote on which artists are right for that show. You often have to submit detailed information about your work and usually need to include photographs of your previous booth displays from other events.

Beyond these resources, your local newspaper is also a great place to start your search. Some newspapers will release listings of the year's regular festivals, which may help you determine which upcoming shows might be a good fit for you.

Small local shows, including school and church bazaars, will often post on Craigslist (*www.craigslist.org*) seeking vendors. The "community – general" and "community – artists" sections seem to be the most popular areas of Craigslist for this type of post.

Craft shows and other events where you can sell your handmade goods come in all shapes and sizes. There are a variety of small-scale local events, like school and church bazaars, as well as long-running festivals and art markets that you can sign up for.

Don't overlook the power of a great Google search either!

Search terms to plug into Google might include (insert your location instead for any of these examples!):

- ➢ "art and craft shows in Florida"
- ➢ "craft shows in Louisiana"
- ➢ "summer art fairs Michigan"
- ➢ "art fairs 2015"
- ➢ "juried art shows in Ohio"
- ➢ "alternative craft fair"
- ➢ "dealer's room anime convention"
- ➢ "steampunk conventions 2016"

You get the idea!

Some of the most popular large indie craft shows include:

- ➢ Art Star Craft Bazaar - Philadelphia, Pennsylvania
  - o www.artstarcraftbazaar.com
- ➢ Cleveland Bazaar - Cleveland, Ohio
  - o www.clevelandbazaar.org
- ➢ Crafty Bastards - Washington, D.C.
  - o www.washingtoncitypaper.com/craftybastards
- ➢ Crafty Wonderland - Portland, Oregon
  - o craftywonderland.com
- ➢ Indie Craft Experience - Atlanta, Georgia

- o www.ice-atlanta.com

- ➤ Renegade Craft Fair - www.renegadecraft.com

    - o Austin, Texas

    - o Chicago, Illinois

    - o Denver, Colorado

    - o London, England

    - o Los Angeles, California

    - o New York, New York

    - o Portland, Oregon

    - o San Francisco, California

    - o Seattle, Washington

- ➤ San Francisco Bazaar - San Francisco, California

    - o www.sanfranciscobazaar.org

- ➤ Stitch Rock - Delray Beach, Florida

    - o www.rockthestitch.com

- ➤ Strange Folk Festival - St. Louis, Missouri

    - o www.strangefolkfestival.com

- ➤ Urban Craft Uprising - Seattle, Washington

    - o www.urbancraftuprising.com

Don't limit yourself to just shows called "craft fairs." Only you will know what markets will be a good fit for your work, but depending on what you make and your personal art style, you might also consider science fiction and fantasy conventions, Renaissance fairs, music festivals, expos geared at moms, home and garden shows, fashion shows and more.

Sometimes you might have to dig around a bit to find vendor applications or organizer contact info. Don't get discouraged! It's a learning process, and once you get started, you'll find it gets easier over time, just like anything else.

3 WHAT TO KNOW BEFORE YOU BOOK A SHOW.

How much should I spend on a booth fee at a show?

Shows can cost anywhere from $10 – $1,000+ to participate in. Some expensive shows won't be worth the money, and some will pay for themselves many times over in terms of sales.

Be smart about your craft show choices and try to learn as much as you can about a show's history, expected attendance and how they advertise their show before you plop down any big bucks.

Some people use the 10x rule to determine if a booth fee is worth it for them, meaning that they want to make 10 times the booth fee back in sales for it to be a good show. For example, if the booth costs $50 to rent, they're hoping to make $500 in sales at that event.

If I can make 5 or 6 times my booth fee, I'm usually pretty happy. But if a booth for a show costs $100, and you make just $250 at that show, after you factor in all of the costs of materials for making your products, plus display materials, and your time and labor, it's not usually worth it.

Things to consider when looking at possible shows

How long has the show been going on? If it's an annual,

monthly or other recurring event, try finding other artists who have sold at this event in the past and see what they thought of it.

For recurring shows, check it out as a customer before you commit to being a vendor. Go to the event as a shopper, but be sure to take note of how many other shoppers there are, and if the shoppers there seem to fit your target market. Also, do people at the show seem to be making a lot of purchases, or are most walking around empty-handed? Ask questions of other vendors there, but also pay attention to their behavior – do they seem bored and uninterested, as if sales have been slow all day?

What is the venue like? Is it an indoor or outdoor event? What is the parking situation like, both for vendors and for customers? Is there an admission fee for customers to attend?

That said, don't rule anything out if you think it will be a good fit for your merchandise! I've spent years experimenting and doing just about any event I think has a good chance at being profitable! A few have been flops, and I'll never go back, but many small shows that I've taken a chance on have been unexpectedly good!

What does "juried craft show" mean?

"Juried" craft show means that any artist interested in participating in the show must apply first. Once all applications have been received, a jury of craft show organizers will assess the applicants and pick those that they think will be the best fit for their show.

Most fine art shows are juried, as well as big shows where there are typically way more people applying than space available.

Many smaller shows are not juried and are first-come, first-serve. There are pros and cons for each type of show. When you are just starting out, it may be hard to get into a juried show. However, the overall quality of the art for sale, as well as the way the show is run by the organizers is often better at juried shows.

How to make your craft show application rock!

Once you start applying to juried craft shows, you'll need to stand out from the crowd.

As you perfect your booth display, whether at other shows or during trial runs at home, be sure to take pictures. Some shows want to see pictures of your booth setup. Also take great shots of your products – clear images taken in natural lighting work best.

A craft show jury, much like your potential customers, wants to know what makes YOU unique. Tell your story in an interesting but concise way. Craft an artist statement about you and your work, but keep it no longer than a brief paragraph. Make sure to include details about how you create your products and what materials you use to do so.

If you've done some shows already, or if you've sold your work in galleries or boutiques, be sure to include a note about that, too. Sometimes this information can make a big impression, and let an organizer know that you're professional and serious about your craft!

Be sure to read the application instructions carefully for each show you apply to, and follow all of the rules! There's no easier way to get on an organizer's bad side than by missing key information on your application.

Questions to consider when booking shows:

Check the registration packets, websites, or ask the promoter these questions to determine if any given show might be a good fit for you.

➢ How many people attended the previous year's show?

➢ How many artists/crafters did you have at the previous show?

➢ How many artists/crafters applied in the previous year, and how many were accepted?

➢ Is the craft show juried?

➢ Does this show allow only art and handmade items, or does it accept other types of products, such as Tupperware or Scentsy?

➢ Does this show limit the number of vendors in any given category? For example, do they limit the number of jewelry vendors?

➢ What is the parking situation for vendors? Is there an additional fee for vendors to park?

➢ Is there a parking fee for customers?

➢ Is there an admission charge for customers?

➢ Is the event indoors or outdoors?

➢ What size is the allotted space?

➢ What is provided with your booth fee? Are a tent, table or chairs included, or will you need to bring your own?

➢ Is there space behind the booth for sitting and/or

storage?

➤ How much will a booth cost to rent?

➤ What are the other costs that may be involved? (Additional application fee, insurance, etc.)

➤ What are the hours of the show?

➤ What time is the earliest or latest you can set up your booth?

➤ What will next year's dates be for this show?

➤ What happens in case of severe weather? Is there a rain date?

➤ Do the artists have to break down each night or is there overnight security for a multi-day show?

➤ Is there an online application, or can you download the application from a website?

➤ Is there a floor plan or map of the show layout available?

➤ If you will be doing the show by yourself, you might ask if there will be any staff on hand to act as booth sitters so you can take a bathroom break or get a bite to eat.

➤ Is there electricity available, and if so, what are the costs and requirements?

➤ If you have special needs, be sure to ask if these can be accommodated. For example, handicap access, parking for a large cargo trailer, etc.

4 HOW TO MAKE YOUR BOOTH LOOK GREAT.

Making a great looking craft show booth display is all about what those in the retail business called "visual merchandising." And let's face it, if you're trying to sell your handmade goods, you're in the retail business.

Visual merchandising includes all the things about how you can make your craft booth look great. That includes how you present your products for display and perusal to help you sell more of them!

Visual merchandising isn't just a realm for only the artistically inclined. In fact, visual merchandising has less to do with artistic talent than one might think – its primary function is to market your business, and to make your store or booth design and layout help your customers find what they need.

Visual merchandising should fulfill your customers' needs as they shop with you. A good booth design and layout will ensure that shoppers can move comfortably and easily throughout the space, and it will allow them to find what they're looking for.

Five visual merchandising basics:

- ➢ company design and brand image
- ➢ layout of your booth
- ➢ fixtures
- ➢ signs
- ➢ how you display individual products

Company design and brand image

Branding is a key part of marketing any business, and your art or craft biz is no different. Your booth design and layout should take all of its cues from your brand image. Some people think that branding means having a good logo. A logo is certainly part of branding, but not all of it.

Think about major chain stores and how their logo, brand image and store designs are all interconnected. Victoria's Secret feels pink and girly, because they sell women's lingerie. GAP feels simple, fresh and modern, as they specialize in classic, basic apparel. Hot Topic tries to sell to edgy teens, so their stores feature lots of dark-colored design elements, and the music they play in their stores is the kind of alternative rock, punk or metal that their target customer listens to.

Layout of your booth

You'll want to create a great flow inside your craft fair booth so that customers can move around easily and shop with comfort. Think about those little things that make you comfortable when you're out shopping – enough mirrors and proper lighting to try on clothing or jewelry, and having products at a height that is not too high or too low to reach with ease.

Limit barriers to entry into your booth, and make sure it's not too crowded. Once, while sharing a booth with another artist for the weekend, we discovered a layout that made it easier for customers to shop.

Previously, we had tried a setup with two large tables on either side of our space, which forced customers to walk into the booth between the tables. The booth quickly felt over-crowded. We noticed that if different people were shopping at each of our tables at the same time, they bumped into each other from behind and would quickly leave after that happened.

Next, we re-arranged our merchandise on two smaller tables, one for each of us, facing outward. We had less space to spread out our products, but the customers could walk directly up to the tables and browse with ease. This new setup allowed us to sell more products.

Always be aware of customer behavior and movement around your booth – adjust as necessary to create a good flow!

Fixtures

Fixtures are what you hang and display your products on. There are tons of ways to do it! You can create all sorts of moveable wall displays with grid-wall fixtures, which are readily available from various supply companies who cater to retail stores. You can also go DIY and build your own.

If you make handmade clothing, you'll probably need some garment racks. Be sure to invest in a sturdy garment rack, preferably with wheels. (A good wheeled garment rack can double as a dolly for loading in and out of a show!) You'll want fixtures that won't blow away during a windy day at an outdoor art market.

Signs

Signs, as well as price tags, are a key part of visual merchandising. Have you ever been in a store that was clearly lacking in signs or price tags and felt frustrated when you couldn't easily find out information about a product? Signs should reflect your shop's brand image in font, color and layout.

You can use signs to make sure people know more about your work and how much it costs. Don't go overboard and clutter up your booth with too many signs. But do use them to inform. (And even to entertain!)

You might also want to buy or make a banner for your booth with your business name and/or website on it so that your booth is instantly recognizable. I sewed my own, but you can also order custom printed banners.

If you accept credit card payments (and you should!), be sure to have a sign indicating this as well.

Signs are great, but be sure to talk to your customers too! People don't always read or notice signs right away, but beyond that, being friendly and talking to your customers is good customer service and will help you sell more.

A simple smile and hello is a great way to start. Try to read your customers – if they seem chatty, try to start a conversation with them, and talk about how you make your work and what inspires it. But if they seem shy and standoffish, give them some space until they engage with you. (But give a smile and hello to every customer, regardless!)

Displaying individual products

How you display items will depend on what you sell and

the type of work you create. Sometimes, big, unique or high-cost items look great displayed alone to make them seem more special. More often than not, booth displays look great when similar objects are grouped together. This rule especially applies to smaller objects. For example, if you sell jewelry, and have a few different areas to display in and you make a few different styles of jewelry, group your displays by style. It will look much more put-together and eye-catching than if you just jumble all of the necklaces together.

You'll want to make your booth look consistent with your brand. For example, the visual look for my brand is colorful, fresh and modern, so I try to make my booth design reflect that. I try to stick to a couple of colors for my displays and props, like tablecloths and bowls. Most of my display items are blue, pink or white. (The notable exception is my green vintage suitcase. But hey – it's awesome and it's an attention getter, so I let that one slide.) The color of my tablecloths is the same color blue as my organza jewelry gift bags that I wrap up purchases in.

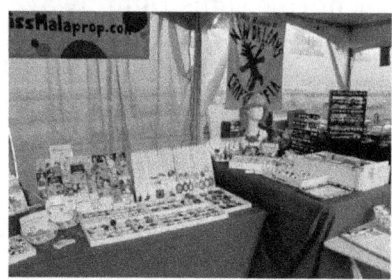 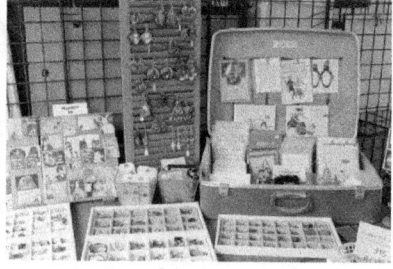

Think back to the work we did to determine your target market and your ideal customer. We can use that same information to help us create a visual brand for our craft show booth.

Is the style of the art you make earthy and rustic? You'll want to use display materials and packaging that reflects that... perhaps materials like wood, burlap and twine will be a part of your displays or the way you gift-wrap your products for customers.

Maybe you create paper goods that are full of simple, clean lines and sharp details. You'll want to set up a booth that goes along with that vibe.

Here are some things you can do to make your booth look killer. How you set up your display will depend on the type of art you make, of course, but use these ideas as a jumping off point. Be creative with your displays – you're an artist after all!

Use levels!

You'll want to draw the eye of your shoppers up and around your booth display. You can do this by using different levels and heights in your booth.

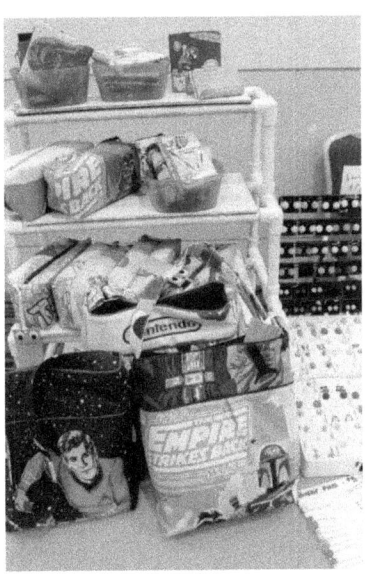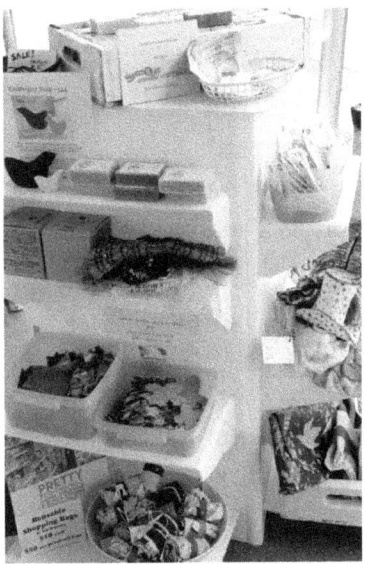

A table where everything is laid out flat isn't nearly as interesting as one that has some things displayed at different heights. There are all sorts of great retail displays you can use to create different levels in your booth.

You can use clear Plexiglas risers to prop up your products at different heights. If you make jewelry, you might lay out some things flat on your table or in portable jewelry trays (which I use to make my setup and breakdown quick and painless), but you should also use some necklace stands or bust-style jewelry displays to add some visual interest.

If you do paintings, prints or fine art, you might create levels on which to hang your work with grid-wall or screens, which you can hang from a standard E-Z UP tent. Mesh screens attached to a tent work great for hanging watercolors or photographic prints. I've seen a lot of fine artists use freestanding mesh display panels to hang their art from as well.

For your tables themselves, you can either get adjustable height tables, or I know some crafters who use risers made for beds to create different heights for their tables.

My boyfriend made me a tiered shelf using PVC pipe and plywood, materials readily available at any hardware store. I used it to display bags made from vintage bedsheets, made by my friend Kendra of Bonga Chop Designs.

Many artists I know use wooden crates as display props and to add height. You can lay them on their side and display things inside, or hang things from the slats. You can also stack more displays on top.

I'm also a big fan of vintage suitcases as display props. I use mine not only to haul stuff to and from the event, but also to create some height and to display greeting cards or other merchandise. I sewed some ribbon by hand into the fabric lining of mine so that I could easily hang stuff from it.

I've also used an old shutter to display hanging earrings. I attached two L-shaped shelf brackets to the back on either side, which I use to clamp it to my table from behind.

Jewelry displays

You may have noticed in the previous pictures on page 20 that I use a lot of trays to display my jewelry. When I started out, I kept everything in small clear bags to transport it to and from the event, and then took it out and laid it on the tables. I quickly learned, however, that this is EXTREMELY time-consuming and it takes forever to set up and break down your booth this way!

Jewelry trays can be a quick and effective way to display and transport your jewelry or other small products. The trays are usually made so that you can order a variety of different inserts with different sized compartments to display your jewelry.

I also use manila shipping tags to display earrings and bobby pins. I hole-punch the tags, add the jewelry and then display them in bowls.

A few neck forms or mannequin heads are great for adding levels and visual interest in your jewelry display, too!

Dressing a mannequin

If you sell clothing, or even jewelry, and plan to use a mannequin in your display, here are a few tips:

Dress your mannequin in the smallest garment that will

fit. If necessary, clip or pin garments so that they fit the mannequin snugly. Your clothing should fit the dress form like a glove.

When accessorizing a mannequin, bigger is better. (But less is more.) Choose bigger necklaces or accessories, as they'll be more eye-catching, and also less easy for anyone to steal unnoticed. But limit your accessories to one or two pieces per mannequin.

Keep it neat!

Be sure to take pride in the appearance of your booth, and keep tidiness in mind. At outdoor shows this can be especially tricky, but keeping certain tools on hand (think wet wipes, napkins and hand sanitizer) can help.

Keeping your booth free of boxes and clutter is not only customer-friendly, but at many shows it's a requirement. Many shows also require that your tent be white, to keep a cohesive look throughout the show, and many craft shows require that you drape your table with a cover or tablecloth all the way to the floor.

Let them try it!

If you sell jewelry, accessories or anything wearable, make sure to bring a mirror, so customers can try before they buy.

For bath or beauty products, have a sample product available to touch, test and smell.

If you make clothing, you might even rig up a portable dressing room. My friend Kendra did this using PVC pipe from the hardware store and curtains.

Give it a trial run

If you've never, ever done a craft show before, and

you're a bit nervous, give it a trial run! Set up your booth at home a few days before your craft show to see if you're missing anything and practice how it will all come together. You might even invite a few friends or family over to give you feedback and do a little pre-show shopping!

Always be on the lookout.

I'm always on the lookout for new inspiration on how to make my display look better. I love to check out other people's booths at shows I do, but of course you should never copy their ideas directly! Let them inspire you to create your own ideas on how to style your booth.

Retail stores with great visual merchandising can be another fabulous source of inspiration. Anthropologie in particular always does an amazing job with their retail displays!

I like to collect my favorite craft show display ideas on Pinterest (*www.pinterest.com/missmalaprop/craft-shows*), and I always love checking out the ideas posted in the Show Me Your Booths group on Flickr (*www.flickr.com/groups/715724@N24/pool*).

Now, let's get started on brainstorming how to make your booth look awesome!

How will your dream craft show booth look?

DO THIS NOW!

> ➤ Close your eyes and imagine the booth of your dreams. What does it look like?
> ➤ Describe the visual style of your products.
> ➤ Pick 3 or 4 colors, at most, that describe your brand.
> o Be specific – not just green, but olive green or emerald green.
> ➤ How big or small are your products?
> ➤ What types of fixtures and displays will you need to make them look great?
> ➤ What signs or price information will you need to include in your booth?
> ➤ When a customer makes a purchase, how will you wrap up your product?
> o Does it need special care or protection?
> o How can you make it look special?

5 PROMOTING YOUR SHOW.

When you're looking into new shows to do, you should always investigate how the show organizers plan to promote their event. How did you first hear about it? Was it via word-of-mouth, from a fellow artist who previously participated in that show, or did you hear about it through some means of advertisement that the organizers did themselves?

It's great to participate in shows where the organizers do a lot of the hard work for you by making sure to get the word out about their show, but you shouldn't just rest on your laurels. It's your responsibility to make sure that your customers know where you'll be and at what shows they can find you. To cover all aspects of marketing your handmade business would be a whole other book. However, here are a few basic tips on what you should be doing to promote yourself and to let people know where and when they can find you at craft shows.

Your website

Whether you have an Etsy shop or a Facebook page for your business, you should also have your own website. A website you set up specifically for your business is something you have ultimate control over. Etsy,

Facebook, or other similar companies can change their rules with a moment's notice. Sites like this also fluctuate in their popularity. Think back to the days when everyone hung out online on MySpace or Friendster. How many people do you know who are currently using these platforms regularly?

Your website can be as simple or complex as you'd like to make it. It can serve as a great hub to direct people to your various social media platforms, and to keep your customers up-to-date on what you're doing. Your website might include a blog, which you can update regularly with new product lines you're working on, or share with your customers where you get your inspiration from. On your website you can also create an events page where you can list your upcoming craft shows so that people can easily see where you'll be.

Your mailing list

Like your own website, your mailing list is something you can have complete control over. Whereas Facebook might change how they show your posts to your customers, you have control over when you send out a newsletter to your mailing list, and what content you include.

Some artists still use old-fashioned snail mail newsletters. There is a certain charm to this and it can be a really nice way to make your customers feel special once in a while. For example, you might send out holiday thank-you cards to your customers who purchased from you online within the past year. If you do this, it's nice to be genuine, friendly and thankful rather than to try to sell something directly through this means of communication. Sometimes it's nice to feel that a company actually appreciates your business and is not always just trying to sell something to you.

On a more regular basis however, email marketing is your best friend. How can you get started in email marketing? When you set up at craft shows, keep a clipboard sign-up sheet or a notebook where customers can leave their name and email address if they're interested in hearing more about your company. You can also create an opt-in for customers who purchase something via your online shop. Make sure not to automatically add people just because they made a purchase with you though. Before you add anyone to your email mailing list, you need to make sure they have specifically given you permission to do so.

For the actual sending out of email newsletters, I'm a big fan of the service called MailChimp (*mailchimp.com*). It's very customizable, pretty easy to learn how to use, and it offers a lot of free and affordable plans for businesses of various sizes.

There are lots of other options as well. Constant Contact (*www.constantcontact.com*) is another email list service frequently used by artists.

Using an email list service is highly recommended. Simply sending out mass emails from your regular email program not only looks unprofessional, but it is also unwieldy and time-consuming to manage. This practice can even get your email address flagged as a spammer and get you blocked by many email providers.

In your emails, you might include some information about what you've been up to with your business, along with a list of any upcoming events and where people can find you. You could also include new products from your online shop, plus links to your website, blog and social media pages.

Create a schedule for yourself to send out email updates on a regular basis, and mark it on your calendar! I recommend sending out an update at least once a month.

Social media

Even though I've already mentioned the importance of having your own website and your own email mailing list, that doesn't mean I don't like social media. Far from it!

Social media sites can be a great tool for growing your handmade business. There are so many good ones, however, they can easily become a time-suck and a distraction. Social media sites can also gain and lose popularity relatively quickly. The sites that are popular one day may not be popular four months from now. So it is important to weigh the benefits of each in relation to your specific business, and make sure that you use your time efficiently when it comes to social media marketing.

My philosophy when it comes to social media is that I will usually sign up for most new sites that look interesting to me, and at least give them a try. If I don't seem to be getting any traffic or interacting with potential new customers or business acquaintances via a social media platform I'll usually back off of it.

For artists and crafters who work in visual mediums, pictures and images can be a big part of growing your social media presence. Images and video on Facebook tend to perform better than text alone. (And multi-image posts or video often tend to get better reach and engagement than a single image in a post!) Instagram, Pinterest, Snapchat or Tumblr are very visual social media platforms that might be a good fit for your business.

There are also lots of tools that make it easy to schedule

some of your social media interactions in advance, which can help limit the amount of time wasted on social media. Facebook offers a useful built-in feature for fan pages that lets you schedule posts for the future. Hootsuite (*hootsuite.com*) is another great tool that can help you schedule posts to Twitter and Facebook as well as other social media platforms in advance. For Instagram, the Later app is super handy for scheduling posts in advance.

6 BE PREPARED:
MY CRAFT SHOW TIPS & TRICKS.

Start with a good tent!

If you'll be doing outdoor shows, a good tent is essential. I'm SO GLAD I invested in an E-Z UP tent right from the start. Some shows require a white tent, which is one of the reasons I went with the E-Z UP, but I've also seen too many other crafters over the years struggle with cheap tents which are often flimsy and harder to set up. (I can, and often do, set up and take down my E-Z UP all by myself.)

In windy conditions, you'll also be glad to have a sturdy tent, paired with a good set of weights. I use the E-Z UP brand weights, stuffed with bricks, but I've seen lots of great DIY options, including water jugs and PVC tent weights. Just make sure your weights are heavy enough to stay put!

I'm also glad my E-Z UP came with a full set of zip-up sides. They're useful not only for rainy days but also for shows that take place over a weekend where you need to leave stuff there overnight.

You can often find E-Z UP brand at local sporting goods stores, or you can order one online.

A hand truck makes life a million times easier.

This is a lesson I've learned the hard way. I went through a couple of cheap dollies, and spent way too much time just carrying everything, before I found the right hand truck. I still have a small Magna Cart hand truck that I use for certain shows, but my boyfriend – the indie filmmaker whiz that he is – changed my life forever when he bought us a top of the line Magliner hand truck to share. I don't know how I'd do some of my art markets without it, as I can finally haul everything I need in one trip.

> Check out my blog post, 5 Craft Show Must Haves, for links to my favorite craft show gear including the E-Z UP tent and hand trucks I personally use: www.missmalaprop.com/5-craft-show-must-haves

Bring your own food and drinks.

I do almost all of my craft shows alone, which makes it hard enough to sneak away to use the restroom, let alone stand in long lines for overpriced festival food. I spent too many shows early on miserable and hungry because I didn't put enough forethought into how and what I would eat during the day.

I now have a small cooler that I bring to all of my shows. Instead of ice, which quickly melts and gets messy, I use a couple of freezer packs to keep things cold. I also have a big water bottle with a built-in freezer stick. This has totally saved me during hot outdoor shows!

I like to bring my own sandwiches and snacks as well, since a lot of food at craft shows and festivals consists of burgers, hot dogs and fried foods. Especially if you have any sort of food allergies, dietary restrictions, or if you just want to eat healthier, it's best to pack your own lunch. I've learned that a foot-long Subway sandwich serves me well on long days, since I can eat half for lunch and still have the other half left over for dinner.

Some festivals like to enforce the "no outside food or drinks" rule. This is legit for regular festival patrons, but as far as I'm concerned, vendors should be exempt from this rule. We pay a lot of money to do the shows, we're stuck there all day, and it's hard to get away from your booth. My cooler is a discreet soft cooler, so it's less obvious than hauling in a giant Igloo ice chest. I've never had a problem, although some shows call for more sneakiness and creativity than others.

Lighting is important!

If you've ever done an outdoor show that goes into the night, or if you've done an indoor show with dim lighting, you'll know what I mean! Christmas string lights are pretty, but they get easily tangled during transport and they are time-consuming to put up around your booth.

A clamp light or two, directed up to bounce light back down from the roof of my white E-Z UP is usually all I need. That, and a good extension cord, of course.

(At Frenchmen Art Market, which is held at night, and where I don't use my tent unless it's raining, my Magliner hand cart usually serves as a light stand to clamp the light to!)

Accept credit cards, and bring plenty of change.

When I first started selling at craft shows in 2004, this was a lot trickier, but in this day and age, there's no excuse not to accept credit cards. Many people don't carry much cash on them, and you're likely to sell more if you can accept credit and debit card transactions.

Square (*squareup.com*) has made it easy and affordable to start accepting credit card payments when doing craft shows, and now even Etsy has gotten in on the game!

The Etsy Reader (*etsy.com/reader*) makes it super easy to integrate your craft show sales with your Etsy shop. The Etsy Reader works similarly to Square, but the sales you make with this app count towards the total number of sales that appear in your Etsy shop. You can also sell items in person that are listed in your Etsy shop, and let it update your inventory automatically, so you never have to worry about overselling something while you're at a craft show.

There are also lots of other options out there as well, including Paypal Here, Propay, and Capital One Bank's Spark Pay program.

Some people still do like to use cash though, and for that reason you should bring plenty of change! How much change? That depends on the show – for all-day festivals where I expect big crowds, I'll bring more change than a smaller show. I usually like to start out with at least $100 in change, including plenty of $1s and $5s.

If I'm going to be doing a show both Saturday and Sunday I'll try to be prepared with more change, since my bank is open only until noon on Saturdays and closed on Sundays.

As for collecting sales tax on cash sales, I just include it in my total price so that I don't have to deal with making coin change and worrying about pennies and nickels and dimes! If you use Square for credit card transactions, it lets you set up a sales tax rate, which it collects on top of the retail price, so you can collect sales tax separately on the credit card transactions.

I've seen some fancy craft show setups that involve a real cash register and everything. That's a bit much for me! I like to keep my change close, with a money apron I made for myself. Lots of craft show vendors keep their money in similar simple tool aprons with pockets that they wear.

Stay comfortable!

Selling at a craft show can make for a long day sometimes. (In a good way!) Wear comfy shoes and clothes that are easy to move around in, load and unload your car in, etc. You'll be on your feet a lot. Some vendors I know have invested in anti-fatigue work mats to stand on behind their booths.

When I do sit down, I like to sit up high so I can still be at eye-level with my standing customers. I went through a couple of cheap fold-up stools before I started getting jealous of other vendors who had fancy folding directors chairs, so I ordered a new tall outdoor director's chair. It's definitely made a difference on long days!

> Check out my blog for a link to where you can buy the chair I use for craft shows: www.missmalaprop.com/the-best-directors-chair

Dealing with crazy weather and unexpected events.

If you ever plan to do outdoor craft shows or festivals, you'll have to be both mentally and physically prepared for some unexpected weather. Nature and all of its elements can be one of the most challenging parts of doing craft shows. I've been at shows with torrential downpours, crazy wind, extreme summer heat and blustery cold nights. It can be very frustrating, don't get me wrong, but sometimes you have to take the good with the bad in order to make a living doing what you love.

Rainy days: tarps, umbrellas and galoshes.

If you plan to do outdoor art markets, your first line of defense against rain is a tent. I have one of the E-Z UP brand tents, which comes with four removable sidewalls. On rainy days, I might put up three out of four sidewalls and leave one wall open so that customers can still come into my booth to shop.

For shows that take place over the course of a weekend where I'm allowed to leave my booth set up overnight, I can put all four sidewalls up, zip them together and leave my booth relatively secure. (Note: I only leave stuff overnight in my booth that I'm okay with risking the chance of it getting stolen or damaged overnight. Even if security is provided at these types of events, it is almost always at your own risk.)

However, what if you're not allowed to have a tent? At one of the local shows I do regularly, Frenchmen Art Market, a few tents are grandfathered in, but generally artists are not allowed to have tents, because of space limitations, and also because of fire codes. This event takes place at night from 7pm until 1am, so sunny days are not a problem.

I do have to make sure to check the weather forecast carefully before I leave the house for this market, and I always come prepared. If even the slightest chance of rain is predicted, I make sure to pack an umbrella, as well as a plastic tarp to throw over my table. I have been at this market when a sudden downpour emerged. All of us artists were in the same boat - we quickly threw tarps over our tables, huddled under umbrellas, and ran and ducked for cover. It sucks, but what can you do?

Some crafts, such as ceramics, are naturally less susceptible to water. If you work primarily with paper products or make handmade soap, or other items that are easily damaged by water, you'll have to weigh the risks accordingly when it comes to setting up at shows where rain is in the forecast.

Even on days that are not rainy, you still need to take water into consideration. What if it rained the night before? The ground might be wet and muddy, so you might need to wear galoshes or rubber shoes, or bring a tarp for the ground so that you and your products don't get covered in mud!

Moisture from fog can also be an issue. On fall and winter evenings where I live, fog is a regular occurrence, so I also keep a towel with me at markets, to wipe off moisture that accumulates on my products before it can damage them.

Windy days and the need for tent weights.

While I do love my E-Z UP tent, on days where it is blustery, the tent has the potential of becoming a wind sail. If you're allowed to set your tent up on a grassy area, you'll want to make sure to bring tent stakes and a hammer to secure your tent. Weights are a must as well. You can purchase weights made specifically for your tent and fill them with sand, bricks or some other heavy material. Some artists also like gallon water jugs, or DIY weights made of PVC pipe from the hardware store filled with sand or cement.

Beyond securing your tent, you'll need to make sure to secure your products as well. If I know it's going to be very windy that day, I will adjust my setup accordingly. While I might normally use a stand-up necklace display, if I know it's going to be very windy on a particular day, I do without the stand-up display, and display my jewelry flat on the table.

Clamps are also your friend on a windy day. Spring

clamps, which are readily available at hardware stores, are a must in my art market toolkit. I keep a bunch of clamps of various sizes available for clamping down my tablecloth to my table legs, and for securing various displays. Binder clips, like those from the office supply store, can also help fasten small items to your tablecloth.

Staying cool on hot days.

I'm from the South, so hot and sunny days are a regular occurrence at art markets that I do. Things tend to slow down around summer due to the extreme heat, but that doesn't mean the art market scene slows down entirely.

Dressing appropriately for the weather is your first line of defense, no matter the forecast. When it's going to be hot outside, make sure to wear comfortable, breathable clothing. Dresses and skirts made of cotton jersey are my favorite thing to wear when it's going to be super-hot outside. I always make sure to bring sunglasses, and if I won't have a tent over my head, I also bring a wide-brimmed hat.

You'll also want to stay hydrated on hot days. I bring a small ice chest with me, packed with lots of water, as well as freezer packs. I preferred these over regular ice because they stayed cold longer and do not get messy when they melt. When it is extremely hot, I'll even take an ice pack out and hold it near my skin, especially on my wrists, inner elbow and on my neck.

Staying warm during cold nights.

For a long time, I sold at the Frenchmen Art Market regularly. It is held at night, and during the winter it gets pretty chilly. Again, dressing appropriately is the first step. I make sure to wear lots of layers since it's not as cold when I'm first setting up as it is later in the night. I love SmartWool and Under Armour brands for creating a barrier of protection against the cold. Some artists bring blankets, maybe even an electric blanket or a heated water bottle. I recently found a bunch of hand warmer packets at my local Target in the dollar section and picked some up to use during especially cold nights.

At this particular art market on super cold nights, they provide outdoor propane heaters. Artists who have their own are also allowed to bring them, although we are restricted on bringing electric heaters due to the electricity regulations and fire codes. However, some art markets during the winter months might allow you to bring your own electric heater so be sure to check with the organizers to see if that's a possibility.

Once again, the food and beverages that I pack can help make the market go a lot smoother when it's cold outside. I have a great Thermos that I keep hot tea in on cold nights. I also pack a to-go mug for coffee, and hot chocolate packets. I've discovered that hot mint tea and instant hot chocolate taste great together!

Keeping potential thieves away.

As much as we don't like to think that anyone would steal from us, shoplifting happens in any sort of retail environment – even craft fairs. It has happened to me (I was more bummed that they stole the display props too, and not just the earrings I had for sale!), and it has happened to both newbie and experienced artists near me at shows.

Don't let one bad apple spoil the whole bunch though – try not to let the thought of possible theft create a bad attitude towards your customers. In fact, great customer service is your first line of defense against shoplifters. Be sure to greet each person that enters your booth as soon as possible. Try to make eye contact with them and give them a friendly smile. Talk to them about the things they're looking at or trying on. Not only is it good salesmanship, it also lets the customer know that you're aware of them, which can deter potential thieves.

If you have a particularly expensive item, keep it closer to you and near the back of the booth. At a recent show, the couple at the booth next to me had an expensive necklace stolen. They had it displayed at the front corner of the booth, making it hard for them to keep an eye on, but easy for a thief to snatch. Try putting less expensive items up front. The larger in size the item, the harder it is to steal, but for very small and expensive pieces, take extra precautions. If you make high-end jewelry, you might even invest in some clear Plexiglas covered display cases.

Be careful not to create blind corners in your booth display, where you can't keep an eye on your merchandise at all times.

Craft Show Supply List

I have one box and one tote bag of stuff that comes with me to every craft show I do. Some of these don't apply to everyone, or to every show, but here is a basic list to get you started:

- ➢ your merchandise!
- ➢ change (coins and small cash bills)
- ➢ money apron or cash box
- ➢ credit card processing equipment
- ➢ E-Z UP tent (for outdoor shows)
- ➢ hand truck / dolly
- ➢ tables and other display materials
- ➢ a tablecloth
- ➢ a chair or stool
- ➢ pen, pencils, permanent markers
- ➢ a notebook for writing down what you sell
- ➢ price stickers or tags
- ➢ extension cord
- ➢ power strip
- ➢ lighting and light bulbs
- ➢ bungee cords
- ➢ zipties or reusable Velcro straps
- ➢ clamps
- ➢ safety pins
- ➢ mirror
- ➢ shopping bags for customers

- wrapping paper or tissue paper for products, if needed
- antibacterial wet wipes and/or hand sanitizer
- toilet paper (especially if you're doing an outdoor show with portable toilets!)
- tape
- rubber bands
- glue
- scissors
- calculator
- business cards
- mailing list sign-up sheets
- sunscreen
- bug spray
- aspirin / ibuprofen / allergy medicine
- a small cooler with water and freezer packs for summer
- a thermos and blanket for winter
- plastic tarp, in case of rain or mud
- umbrella

7 HOW TO GIVE GREAT CUSTOMER SERVICE!

Have you ever been to a craft show and seen artists behind their booths, slumped in a chair, reading a book or checking their phone, looking totally bored and uninterested in selling their art? Did it make you want to buy anything, or even investigate further? Probably not!

Being a great salesperson and giving good customer service go hand in hand. Selling equals helping!

First, when a customer approaches your booth, be sure to smile and greet them in a friendly way. A simple "Hello!" is great!

I always try to get a sense of the customer's personality and go from there. If the customer seems really friendly and chatty, I'll start talking with them about an item that they might be looking at, or explain a little bit about my process and my work. But if a customer seems very shy or standoffish, I try to give them a little bit of space and let them look at their own leisure.

People usually go to craft shows and art markets because they love to hear the stories behind the work and meet the people who made the products. Artists are often shy and introverted by nature. (I know I am!) Learning how to be a little outgoing will go a long way in selling more of your work.

If you're very shy and have trouble talking about your work, you might want to practice at home with a friend or family member that you trust. Have them pretend to be a customer and practice some scripts that you can use when you're at the craft shows. You might even want to have a friend who is a little more outgoing come with you and help you when you do the craft show.

Selling your work at a craft show can go beyond just talking about how you made it or what inspired the piece. Especially if you're selling at a show around the holidays, customers are probably searching for gifts. You might be able to help them by asking them questions about the person that they are gift shopping for. What does that person like? What colors do they like or dislike?

Maybe there are ways that you can customize some of your work, and even charge a little extra money for the customization. If you make jewelry, perhaps you can bring some wire cutters and jewelry pliers and offer to shorten or lengthen necklace chains during an event, as long as you are not busy with other customers.

If you are an artist selling prints, you might even wait until the customer makes a purchase to sign the print in front of them, to make their experience that much more special!

Making life-long customers.

The reason to give great customer service and to create customer-friendly policies is the "lifetime value of a customer." Some customers will only purchase from you once. But hopefully you will have quite a few who will come back more than once. And hopefully, these happy customers will tell their friends about you, who will also become your customers.

Likewise – unhappy customers are even more likely to tell their friends about their bad experiences. Think about it:

when you are really pissed off, aren't you more likely to complain and tell everyone you know who will listen than when you are simply satisfied?

One basic financial principle is the power of compound interest. It works for you when your money is in an interest-bearing account: save $100 in an account earning 5% interest, and at the end of the month you'll have $105. You made 5 bucks! Don't do anything and the next month you'll earn $5.25 in interest instead, bringing your total to $110.25. I think the beauty of compound interest has a lot in common with the idea of "lifetime value of a customer."

Treat a customer decently, and they might come back to you. Go out of your way to be helpful and courteous, and you stand a greater chance that they'll spend money with you again. Each new customer costs you money – you have to spend time and money marketing and finding them, right? Each customer that keeps coming back for more means that you didn't have to spend as much time or money finding them after their first purchase. Less time and money on marketing, more returning, happy customers means more profit for you!

Don't let a bad experience with a crazy customer or a shipping nightmare caused by the post office force you to create customer un-friendly policies.

You should think about common customer service questions and problems and how you want to deal with them, and write a set of policies for your business, even if it's just for your own personal reference. Look to some of the big boys who have been successful in customer service – both Amazon and Zappos are well-known for their customer-friendly policies. Some of what they do may not work for you, but how can you apply what they do to your own business?

Do you currently have any customer un-friendly policies? If

so, why were they created? Was it a bad experience or because you saw other companies post similar policies?

How can you adapt your current policies to offer alternative ways to satisfy your customer, whether they might want a refund or exchange? Maybe if they want a refund, you can offer them store credit plus a little something extra, as an incentive to keep them as a customer.

Dress the part!

If you make something wearable, like jewelry, hair accessories or clothing, be sure to be your own model and wear some of your own creations!

While you must dress for the weather when doing outdoor events, also try to dress the part to go along with your art. If you sell super feminine feather hairpieces or girly jewelry, you probably don't want to wear a trucker hat and flannel shirt to your next show!

Dress to impress as much as possible, but in a creative way that expresses the art you make and sell.

A good attitude is everything!

Having a good attitude about the event can help you sell more! (It will also make your day go by faster!)

If you shut down your booth before the advertised hours of the show end, you're not only missing last-minute customers (sometimes the majority of my own sales have come in the last hour of a show), but you're also being rude to all of the other vendors around you who want to stay open during the entire time that they are supposed to.

Shutting down early sends a signal to shoppers that the show is ending, whether it is the official end time or not. This affects not just you and your sales, but all of the other vendors around you.

Be kind and courteous, and respectful of your fellow vendors, the craft show organizers, and most of all, your customers.

Make your customers happy.

DO THIS NOW!

> ➤ Do you currently have any customer un-friendly policies? If so, what are they?
> ➤ Why did you create these policies?
> ➤ What policies do you currently have in place that are customer-friendly?
> ➤ How can you improve these policies to go the extra mile for your customers?
> ➤ Do you currently have repeat customers? Name your 5 best customers.
> ➤ How can you make these 5 best customers feel extra special?

8 HOW TO SELL MORE.

What sells at craft shows?

I can't tell you what to create, but no matter what your art, you'll want to create a few different price points of products. For example, a painter who might charge $2,000 for an original painting that took her months to create could also offer lithograph prints of that same painting for $50. She might also offer a boxed set of greeting cards featuring the same image for $9 a set, or magnets printed with the image for $5 each.

Having some high-priced offerings is good, because it increases your overall revenue. But also having mid-range, as well as inexpensive impulse purchase items will help you appeal to different segments of your audience, and drive more sales. People might be willing to spend big bucks on themselves, but they might have a set budget for gift-giving. (Or vice versa!)

Bundling your products to sell more.

For popular products that are not one-of-a-kind, and that you can create in bulk and sell large quantities of, you might also consider bundling.

For example, I sell a lot of earrings, most of which are priced at $12 each. But at local craft shows, I offer a special price of 2 pairs for $20. I know my costs, and I'm still making money by offering them this way. People often buy that second pair when otherwise they might have walked away with just one pair of earrings. Plus, I don't even have to break a twenty-dollar bill to make change!

Another form of bundling is where you might offer products that naturally go together as a pre-bundled set. For example:

A fine artist might have 3 prints in a series that they could sell for a slightly discounted price if someone wants to purchase all three at the same time.

A soap maker might create a gift set with a few of their most popular soaps, plus a soap dish and scrub brush, all packaged ready for gift-giving.

Think about ways you might be able to bundle some of your current offerings together to add more value for your customers and make their life easier. Think about ways that bundling can create add-on sales and increase your profits!

How to use craft shows to create after-the-show sales.

I always try to think of the value of any given show as more than just the actual cash money that I made that day. Getting your products out there and meeting people face-to-face is, in my opinion, the absolute best way to market your business.

If you sell only on Etsy or via your own online shop, it can be really hard to get your work seen in a sea of so many handmade products and shiny things to look at. Surely, if you've ever explored Etsy or any other online marketplace, you quickly realized how distracting it can be. There's just so much cool stuff to look at, so it can be really overwhelming.

While a craft show can sometimes be equally overwhelming, you also have the chance to make a much bigger, and more lasting impression. You can literally tell the stories about what inspired your products and talk to customers face-to-face about the process that you went through to create them. Customers can see and touch your products. There is also value in the customer's need for instant gratification at a craft show. The customer can decide to splurge on one of your products and take it home immediately, which can be so much more exciting than when they have to order something online and wait days for it to arrive in the mail.

Even when customers aren't ready to buy something right away, I always treat them just the same, with a friendly attitude. I make sure to give them a business card and tell them that they can shop online, and find me on Facebook. If you have a mailing list (which I highly recommend), you can keep a sign-up sheet on your table so that customers can stay up-to-date with where you'll be and when to check out new product offerings on your website.

If you're interested in selling wholesale or on consignment with retail shops and boutiques, craft shows can also be a great way to meet shop owners. Savvy boutique owners who are looking for unique products will often come to shows to find cool handmade artisan goods.

When a customer makes a purchase from me at a show, I always include a business card in their bag.

You might also want to add a special discount code that they can use after the show to redeem on orders from your online shop. This can also be a helpful tool for tracking which shows were successful in terms of after-the-show sales if you create a different code for each event. Try printing event-specific coupon codes using printable address label stickers, and attach the stickers to the back of your business cards.

If you want to get really fancy, you can even create a QR code that customers can scan with their smart phone, and you can set it up to send them to your website or to a sign-up page for your mailing list. You can Google search "QR code generator" to find easy and free options to do this with.

Make a photo book or portfolio to show off custom creations.

If you make lots of one-of-a-kind or custom pieces, make a photo book or portfolio with examples of your past work. You can use a simple binder or scrapbook, and print out images of past creations.

I have many friends who do this, and it is a great way to let people know that you are available for future commissions. It's a good tool to generate sales long after the craft show is over.

9 GOING BEYOND TRADITIONAL CRAFT SHOWS.

Alternative venues to sell your work.

Many of my fellow artist friends and creative types have moved beyond the traditional craft shows as a means to sell their work. I myself have also experimented with many different types of venues in order to get my products out there.

For example, my friends Brian and Gwen have a T-shirt company called Sigh Co. Graphics (*www.sighco.com*). They create original designs and do all of the screen-printing themselves. Their subject matter, however, does not usually fit in at mainstream craft shows. Their interests are in early 20th-century horror author H.P. Lovecraft, as well as gothic, steampunk and other spooky and alternative themes. In addition to selling their work online, they vend primarily at science fiction and horror conventions. They sell at huge annual conventions like San Diego Comic Con, and now they even run the H.P. Lovecraft Film Festival in their home base of Portland, Oregon.

On occasion I've even sold at science fiction or anime conventions myself, even though my jewelry and other products aren't specifically science fiction themed. However, because my style is a little bit more kitschy and alternative, I've found that the audiences at these types of shows are often more receptive to the work I do than the audience at a traditional church craft fair.

My friend Marrus (*www.marrusart.com*), who is an extremely talented visual artist, does a variety of shows as well. She's been making a living at it for over 20 years now. While she does sell at the Frenchmen Art Market, a weekly nighttime market here in New Orleans, she's also found great success at alternative venues such as fetish conventions and Renaissance festivals. She's found that her work speaks to people who often attend these events.

Both Marrus and Brian and Gwen have done a great job of using these alternative events as advertisement for their businesses. People who find them at these events often become return customers who order again and again from them via their online stores.

Branching out to alternative events goes back to thinking about your target customer. If the work that you are creating reflects yourself, which it often does, then the people who will be into the kind of work you do will probably be at the types of events that you would like to attend yourself. I'm kind of a geek, therefore I've found some success while selling at geeky conventions.

I've also experimented with selling my work at flea markets. This is primarily due to the fact that my mom owns a large outdoor flea market, which makes it easy for me to test out that venue. I've found that my work is a bit too edgy for the crowd that comes to her flea market. But this doesn't mean that flea markets might not be a great place for your work.

Flea markets, what sells well at them, and the types of customers they attract tends to vary a lot depending on your area. Some might be more upscale than others, or have lots of handmade artisans. While my work doesn't sell very well at the flea market my mom owns, I do know many artists whose work does.

Vendors specializing in more traditional crafts like woodworking often do very well at flea markets. Handcrafted body products and soaps, as well as canned or pickled food goods, also usually do well at a flea market.

Create your own events.

Since the types of events that I like to do and that my products sell well at don't always readily exist in my area, sometimes I have to take matters into my own hands and create an event!

I've partnered with fellow crafters to set up a variety of different events over the years. In 2005, I joined forces with a few like-minded local crafters to start the New Orleans Craft Mafia. We based our group off of a similar organization from Austin, Texas. Over the years we hosted many events, including a popular annual holiday art market we called the Last Stop Shop.

If you sell your goods wholesale or do consignment with a local boutique, holding a trunk show in their store can be a win-win for both of your businesses. It allows you some face time with the shop's customers, and the store gets to promote a fun "meet-the-artist" event to the local media!

Sometimes trunk shows might tie in to other local activities, like a monthly art walk or a Fashion's Night Out type of event that you can piggyback on for publicity. You can also make your trunk show an exclusive after-hours event for the shop's VIP customers to reward them for their loyalty.

Don't currently sell to any boutiques? Think about other types of businesses or existing events to partner with. For example, a handmade jewelry line might partner well with a beauty salon for a trunk show event. In the past, I've partnered with friends who owned local businesses to host trunk shows and "pop-up shops" at their locations. My friend who ran a day spa and yoga studio once hosted a trunk show for me, and another time I did a pop-up event at a different friend's guitar shop which was located on a busy street in the French Quarter.

One year, I partnered with another local artist to sublet our friend's art studio on Magazine Street, which is a popular location for shops here in New Orleans. The space was typically used to teach art classes to kids, but during the holidays she allowed us to rent out the location from her for a couple of weekends and transform it into a limited edition holiday boutique.

Be sure to think about your target audience when brainstorming possible collaborations. My friends Hope and Nico own a lady-friendly, education-focused "adult" boutique named Dynamo (*shop.dynamotoys.com*). They came to me early on for business advice, and I suggested partnering with local burlesque shows to sell their goods during events, since the audience at those shows were a natural fit for their products.

Publicizing your own events.

Whenever you are organizing an event at a public venue, you'll need to make sure to promote it. Give yourself plenty of time to publicize the event and let people know about it.

Over the years, the New Orleans Craft Mafia hosted many of our own events and we built a great following locally. While we're no longer actively organizing events as a group, I learned a lot from the process.

Each time we scheduled an event, we wrote and sent out a press release via email to local newspapers, T.V. stations and blogs. Never underestimate the power of sending out a press release, especially if you can make your event sound interesting and exciting. You can search online for press release templates if you've never written one, but be sure to include the what, why, when, where and who of your event. Include all of the information that a news sources would possibly need to know if they were to feature you. You'll also want to consider the "human interest" side of things. What makes your event special or different?

Don't forget to let your existing customers know about your event via your email list and social media.

Host a home shopping party!

Another type of event I sold my crafty goods at was the home shopping party, modeled after Tupperware or Mary Kay parties. I hosted the first party at my house in October 2009, and a few weeks later my friend Leslie hosted a party for me at a coffee shop here in New Orleans.

Here are a few tips on getting started with selling your handmade art via home shopping parties:

Give your host great incentives!

After scouting some tips online, I decided to offer $25 in shop credit plus 10% of my total sales as shop credit to the hosts of my parties. If you make mainly one type of item, like jewelry or handbags, you might want to offer the host their choice of a certain type of earring or clutch, but since I carry such a wide variety of products, I thought that shop credit would be the easiest way to go.

Think of these incentives as you would a booth fee at your local craft fair. The great part is that, unlike a craft fair, where you pay your fee and then have to make your money back, here you offer the hostess a percentage of your sales as shop credit. If she brings in lots of friends who buy lots of stuff, she does well too and gets freebies from you, but if the party ends up being a bust, you're not out a ton of money. (But from my own experience, and the stories I've heard from more experienced handmade home shopping party aficionados, you're more likely to do very well than not!)

Make it fun!

It's a party, so treat it like one! Whether you're hosting the party at your own home, a friend is hosting at theirs or you do it at a coffee shop like the party my friend Leslie set up, make sure there are plenty of drinks and snacks available! The coffee shop we partnered with loved us because we brought new customers into their shop. At my first home party that I hosted I made sure there was plenty of wine and cheese to go around. Drinks and snacks can be as cheap or as expensive as you'd like... Each party could have a slightly different theme, depending on the host's preferences.

Taking a cue from Tupperware parties that I had been to, I also made sure to create some fun and excitement with giveaways! You can pick out a few lower-priced items to give away or do a drawing for $10 in shop credit. You can also create fun games or even do a demonstration of how you make your craft. People will see the work and talent it takes to create your items and they just might be more inclined to buy!

Communicate your needs for setup!

The first party I did was at my house, so I had all day to get my setup just right and use whatever random materials I had around the house for displaying my goods. I invited other artist friends to set up in my home as well, and while we were worried at first how to make everything fit, by using furniture already in my home, we made it work. We accidentally scratched our credenza though, so whether at your home or someone else's, if you're going to use someone's furniture to display your goods, make sure to throw a tablecloth over it first! That's one of those little things that didn't even occur to me but in hindsight I wish I had thought of it before we scratched up the furniture!

For my second event at the coffee shop, my friend Tressa and I both set up for the party. Leslie, who had arranged things with the coffee shop manager, had given us details about the space and timing of setup. Tressa and I were both a little worried, because we thought we were only being allowed 30 minutes to set up. (I typically take about an hour or so to feel comfortable with my set up.) Luckily it all worked out though... I arrived early to scope out the space and have some coffee. The manager introduced himself to me and not only let us set up earlier than we thought, but he also helped us move tables and even ran home to get us extra lighting! In the future, I'll make sure to clarify that I need at least an hour or so before guests arrive to set up my goods, so there's no need to stress!

Get their contact info!

As I mentioned above, we did some fun giveaways, and the way I had people enter the drawing was to fill out a slip of paper with their contact info, including their name, email address and phone number.

I included lines asking if they would like to be included on my email newsletter list and if they were interested in possibly hosting a handmade home shopping party of their own. On the form I asked, if the answer is yes, what day and time do they have in mind? I also left a blank for any additional comments or suggestions.

This is your captive audience... they're already interested in what you do, so don't miss the opportunity to stay in touch with them!

Additional types of events to help grow your crafty business:

Teaching Workshops and Demonstrations

This type of event is more about building your brand and positioning yourself as an expert in your field than for direct selling. However, you can also easily combine this type of event with a trunk show or home shopping party. Typically projects you teach should be easy enough for beginners. You won't want to show them how to make your best-sellers, but give them an easy project to do that will make them appreciate just how much hard work and skill goes into each of your creations. You might do educational demonstrations for free at first, but later on you might add paid teaching gigs to your crafty income streams.

Business Networking and Mastermind Groups

This event type is also more about building your brand than direct selling to consumers. At networking events and through mastermind groups made up of your business peers, you'll meet the people you can collaborate with on future projects and events. These people can also help support and guide you in aspects of your business where you may feel weak – and you might be able to help them in aspects that are your strength. Where you find "your people" will depend on your type of business, but a Chamber of Commerce or a local LinkedIn, Facebook or Etsy group for savvy business owners can be a good start to finding local business owners to connect with.

10 GETTING LEGIT AND STAYING ORGANIZED.

Legalities, licenses, taxes and fees.

I live in New Orleans, Louisiana, so my experience is mostly with the laws in this area, and in the United States. The licenses and requirements vary greatly from area to area, even within the U.S., let alone outside of this country. However, in most areas, a quick search on Google can get you started in figuring out what is needed to get legal in your area.

If you have an accountant, especially one who works with businesses, they can often be a great asset and can help you determine what you need to do to get squared away. Many universities and even community colleges also have programs to help small businesses in their areas. Take advantage of any of these opportunities, as they will be well-versed in your local laws.

Many well-established and bigger craft shows will also be able to inform you of any special requirements for filing sales tax for their show, or any other special paperwork you might need, such as insurance.

Often, when I've done a show away from home, whether in a different state or county, the organizers of the show have been very helpful with providing details on how to pay my sales tax for that show and what licenses I need for the show. Be sure to check with the craft fair organizers when in doubt!

Within the U.S., the Small Business Association offers many helpful resources on their website (www.sba.gov).

Stay organized: tracking your inventory.

Staying organized and on top of your inventory is a must. I use Microsoft Excel to keep track of all of my inventory, as well as my retail prices and cost information. I also use this document to organize the information on where I get my supplies for each product. Google Docs is a great free resource that's easy to use if you don't have access to Excel.

	A	B	C	E
1	Item #	description	retail price	Inventory
2				
3			$12.00	2
4				
5	MM_ring013	raspberry honeycomb	$12.00	4
6				
7	MM_ring014	oval nouveau floral cameo - assorted colors	$12.00	10
8	MM_ring015	Skeleton cameo ring - small - ivory on black	$12.00	4
9	MM_ring016	Skeleton cameo ring - small - assorted colors	$12.00	6
10				
11	MM_ring017a	Owl head, small necklace, blue	$12.00	3
12	MM_ring017b	Owl head, small necklace, red	$12.00	4
13				
14	MM_ring018	large cameo ring - lady face - assorted	$14.00	3
15				
16				
17	MM_ring032	oval resin floral cluster rings - assorted	$10.00	11
18				
19	MM_ring034	miscellanous floral rings	$10.00	69

Above is an example of how I keep track of my inventory. This is just a small portion of the information I include in my document. You'll need to figure out a system that works best for you and your products, but this is what I do:

- ➢ Within Excel, I have separate worksheets for each type of product. For example, this is just a snapshot of my inventory worksheet for rings.

- ➢ I assign each item an individual number, and I use jewelry tags on each product to keep track of their item numbers and their prices. This also makes it easy for customers to see the prices for each product while they are shopping. My company is called Miss Malaprop, so I start all of my inventory numbers with MM. All rings start with the item number MMR, followed by a three digit number which I assign in consecutive order. (In my Excel document, I write out MM_ring, but on my jewelry tags I use the abbreviation MMR.)

➢ I use MM at the beginning of the item numbers for products I make, because I also sell products made by other artists as well. The products made by those artists all get their own abbreviations to help me know who made what. If you're only selling your own work, you might just use abbreviations to let you know what type of product it is ... Maybe RR for rings and NN for necklaces, followed by a number.

➢ In my document, I include a column for the item numbers, a column for the description of the products, a column for the retail price, a column for the cost of each product (which I have hidden here), and a column for the amount of each product I have in inventory.

➢ I also have columns where I can keep track of which supply source I used to find the parts to make each product. Some suppliers have their own product numbers, so I also have a column where I keep track of those numbers to make it easier to reorder supplies.

Obviously you'll need to figure out a system that works for you, but in the example above, I've used black normal text for products which I currently have in stock, and change the font to light gray when I run out of that product. The line that is highlighted in blue lets me know that that product is already listed on my website. This helps me know that if I run out of that product I'll need to update my website accordingly and remove that product from my online shop.

For keeping track of what I sell during the craft show itself, I use a regular notebook. For each day I create a separate page. At the top of the page I write what the event is and the day's date. I also make notes to myself up top about how much cash change I brought that day, and what the booth fee was for that show.

If I'm doing a show that takes place over the course of a weekend, or multiple days, I still do separate inventory pages for each day of the show, because I like to balance out my cash totals at the end of each day, and pull out any large cash bills at the end of each day.

As I sell products throughout the show, I write any item numbers and if necessary, a short description of the product. Along the right-hand side of the page I write the price that I sold the item for and whether it was a cash sale or credit card sale (I use a CC as shorthand for credit card). Sometimes I might even get a check from a customer, which I will note in the column. Likewise, on the rare occasion that I do a trade with another vendor, or if something gets broken or damaged, I make a note of that item's number and description and write that it was damaged so that I will remember to take it out of my Excel inventory once I get back home.

When I get home, either after the show or the next day, I first add up my sales totals. This is when I get the numbers that you see at the bottom of the page. I total all of my cash sales, and I total all of my credit card sales. I also get a grand total which is the number circled in red. Once I have my cash total figured out, I count my money. This is where keeping track of how much change I started the day with comes in handy. In this example, I should have $370 total in cash, since I started the day with $125 in change, and made $245 in cash sales.

After I check my totals, I also enter my total sales amount

into a separate Excel document where I keep track of my monthly sales and business expenses. This document is based on one given to me by my accountant.

Now it's time to update my inventory. I'll open up my inventory spreadsheet in Excel, and change the number of items I have in stock based on what I've sold. As I update the numbers in my Excel spreadsheet, I check the items off with a red pen along the left side of the page.

That's pretty much it! There are fancier ways of tracking inventory of course, but this simple system has worked for me for a number of years now.

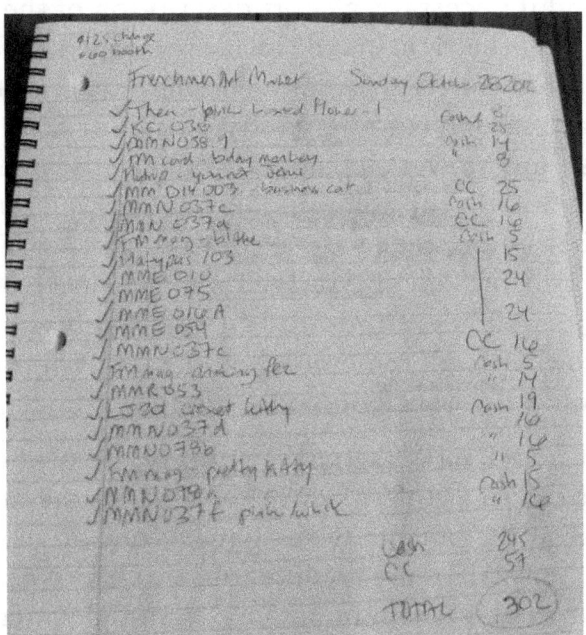

11 CAN I MAKE A LIVING SELLING AT CRAFT SHOWS?

Most artists or crafters who make a living at their craft do so through multiple streams of income. That means, while they may make a large chunk of their income via selling at craft shows, they probably also make money from selling online, or selling wholesale or via consignment to boutiques or art galleries. They might make a big part of their income via craft shows, but they might also have a part-time job in addition for a more steady income stream.

Check out this post on my blog for more info and tips on making a living as an artist: www.missmalaprop.com/how-to-make-a-living-as-an-artist-crafter

Yes, you CAN make a living selling at craft shows, but if you're a smart artist, you'll learn to diversify your income streams, so that you're never stuck wondering where your next meal or mortgage payment is coming from. Selling at art markets will create a variable income, meaning that one day you might make $1,000 at a show, and the next day you might make $75. You'll want to create and stick to a budget, and make sure that you have an emergency savings cushion in case of slow times.

Let's figure out exactly how much it costs you to live each month, and exactly how much it costs to run your business.

Create a personal spending plan.

DO THIS NOW!

- ➤ Let's figure out exactly what it costs you to get by each MONTH. We'll make sure all expenses are covered!
- ➤ List all of the personal expenses you MUST pay, i.e. rent, utilities, debt payments, etc.
- ➤ List your personal monthly expenses that make life fun – gym membership, date night, etc.
- ➤ List the stuff that comes up over the course of a year, add it all up and divide by 12 to get a monthly average – doctor's visits, vet bills, car repairs, insurance payments, etc.
- ➤ List your monthly expenses you can budget but that still need to be taken care of – groceries, retirement contributions, cable TV bill, Internet, etc.
- ➤ If you're not sure, guess the amounts, but guess on the HIGH side. Add it all up to get a monthly total for the minimum amount your business needs to bring in each month to pay your personal bills!
- ➤ Write down the total amount of your personal spending plan.

Create a business spending plan.

DO THIS NOW!

- ➢ Now let's determine exactly what your business costs to run each MONTH.
- ➢ List all of the business expenses you MUST pay, i.e. rent, utilities, debt payments, etc.
- ➢ List the necessary things to run your business, i.e. payroll, advertising, etc.
- ➢ List things that you can control costs for but that still need to be paid, such as office supplies, vehicle expenses, craft show booth fees, etc.
- ➢ Insert the total amount from your personal spending plan, on the previous page.
- ➢ If you're not sure, guess the amounts, but guess on the HIGH side. Add it all up to get a monthly total for the minimum amount your business needs to bring in each month to cover your expenses. This does NOT include your inventory cost (your cost of goods sold), taxes or profit.
- ➢ Write down the total amount of your business spending plan.

Create a business income plan.

DO THIS NOW!

> ➢ Write down the total amount of your business spending plan from the previous page. (Remember that it also includes the total amount of your personal spending plan!)
> ➢ Set aside money for your income taxes (here in the U.S., aim for around 30% of your net income to be safe).
> ➢ Make sure you have money for profit! 20% of your total income is a great goal!
> ➢ And don't forget about the cost of goods sold, the expense that it costs to create the products that you sell.
> ➢ Add these numbers up to get your business income plan. This will be the total amount of money your business needs to make each month in order to sustain itself and you!

I highly recommend consulting an accountant before embarking into the world of full-time craft show self-employment. The above worksheets are based on information given to me by an accountant friend, but should not replace professional advice from an accountant who knows your individual needs and situation.

If possible, consult with a professional early on. Try to find someone who specializes in working with businesses, and even better – find someone who specializes in creative businesses.

They should be able to explain basic tools like a profit and loss report and an income statement, and they should help you get set up to keep track of your income and expenses. There are many free and inexpensive tools available to keep track of this information with, and some work better for different types of businesses. That is why consulting early on with a professional is very important.

Good luck at your next craft show!

I hope you've found this book useful! Craft shows are a lot of fun – a lot of hard work, too, but definitely worth the effort!

After reading this book, and checking out the resources on the following pages, if you still have any craft show related questions, please let me know! I'd be happy to answer any questions you still have.

You can email me directly at Mallory@missmalaprop.com

Good luck, have fun, and make lots of money at your next craft show!

Xoxo,

Mallory

P.S. I would love it if you could leave a review for this book on Amazon! It helps me out a lot. Thank you!!

BIG HUNKIN' LIST OF CRAFT SHOW RESOURCES.

My post on how to make a living as an artist or crafter:

➤ www.missmalaprop.com/how-to-make-a-living-as-an-artist-crafter

Where to find shows:

➤ Art Fair Calendar (*artfaircalendar.com*)

➤ Art Fair Insiders (*www.artfairinsiders.com*)

➤ Craftlister (*www.craftlister.com*)

➤ Craftmaster News (*www.craftmasternews.com*)

➤ Fairs and Festivals (*www.fairsandfestivals.net*)

➤ Festival Network Online (*festivalnet.com*)

➤ Master Craft Show List (*etsy.com/teams/7450/master-craft-show-list*)

➤ SciFiConventions.com (*www.scificonventions.com*)

➤ Sugarloaf Craft Festivals (*www.sugarloafcrafts.com*)

➤ Sunshine Artist (*sunshineartist.com*)

➤ Unanimous Craft (*www.unanimouscraft.com*)

➤ UpcomingCons (*www.upcomingcons.com*)

➤ ZAPP (*www.zapplication.org*)

How to take credit and debit cards at craft shows:

- ➤ Square (*squareup.com*)

- ➤ Etsy Reader (*etsy.com/reader*)

- ➤ Intuit GoPayment (*payments.intuit.com/mobile-credit-card-processing*)

- ➤ ProPay (*propay.com*)

- ➤ Paypal Here (*paypal.com/webapps/mpp/credit-card-reader*)

- ➤ Spark Pay by Capital One Bank (*sparkpay.com*)

Booth display ideas:

- ➤ Visual Merchandising Tips and Tricks (*www.missmalaprop.com/craft-show-display-tips-tricks*)

- ➤ My favorite craft show displays (*pinterest.com/missmalaprop/craft-shows*)

- ➤ Show Me Your Booths group on Flickr (*flickr.com/groups/715724@N24/pool*)

Booth display equipment and props:

- ➤ My craft show must haves, with links to purchase the items I've talked about in this book: (*www.missmalaprop.com/5-craft-show-must-haves*)

- ➤ JewelBox Display & Supply Co, jewelry display supplies (*jewelboxco.com*)

- ➤ Firefly Store Solutions (*fireflystoresolutions.com*)

- ➤ Store Supply Warehouse (*www.storesupply.com*)

- ➤ DIY tent weights tutorial (*http://www.artfairinsiders.com/forum/topics/how-to-make-weights-for-your-tent-for-less-than-30-2*)

Packaging and gift wrap supplies:

- ➤ Nashville Wraps (*nashvillewraps.com*)

- ➤ Uline (*www.uline.com*)

Marketing and how to get the word out:

- ➤ MailChimp (*mailchimp.com*)

- ➤ Constant Contact (*www.constantcontact.com*)

- ➤ Hootsuite (*hootsuite.com*)

- ➤ Later, formerly Latergramme (*later.com*)

- ➤ 99 Ways to Market Your Art - Copyblogger

  (*copyblogger.com/art-marketing*)

- ➤ Email Marketing: How to Push Send and Grow Your Business

  (*copyblogger.com/email-marketing*)

- ➤ Ramit Sethi and Chase Jarvis video, on what it takes to be successful as an artist (*http://bit.ly/ramitchase*)

All around creative business awesomeness:

- ➤ biz ladies, Design*Sponge (*designsponge.com/category/biz-ladies*)

- ➤ Create & Thrive (*createandthrive.com*)

- ➤ Designing an MBA (*designinganmba.com*)

- ➤ Handmadeology (*handmadeology.com*)

- ➤ IndieMade (*indiemade.com*)

- ➤ Smaller Box (*smallerbox.net*)

- ➤ Tara Gentile (*www.taragentile.com*)

And of course.... My stuff!

Find me and more resources at:

- ➤ *MissMalaprop.com*

Join my free community of artists and creative entrepreneurs:

- ➤ *facebook.com/groups/badasscreatives*

ABOUT THE AUTHOR

Mallory Whitfield has been blogging at MissMalaprop.com since 2006. Throughout her journey as a creative entrepreneur, Mallory has worn many hats, including blogger, visual artist, upcycled clothing creator, performance artist, jewelry designer, craft show vendor, creative strategist, speaker, teacher and consultant to other small business owners. By day, she specializes in SEO, social media, and content marketing at FSC Interactive, a leading digital marketing agency in New Orleans.

www.ingramcontent.com/pod-product-compliance
Lightning Source LLC
Chambersburg PA
CBHW060408190526
45169CB00002B/808